Praise for *Giving Back* . . .

"Over the past 10 years I have seen so many women who truly believed that THEY were the only victim of their crime. After a class, they come away with a realization and new attitude about what they have done and how many people were affected. The class is one of the single most effective things I have seen done at Nebraska Correctional Center for Women."

~ **Mary Alley**
Victims Advocate Teacher II,
Nebraska Correctional Center for Women

"This is an inspiring story that translated to helping thousands of individuals. Our evaluation shows that Jim's journey has real-life results. This treatment is a first line treatment for all going through the judicial system."

~ **Dennis E. McChargue, Ph.D.**
Associate Professor, Psychology Department, University of
Nebraska-Lincoln

"As a judge who has been using the accountability class in my juvenile cases, I have found this class to be invaluable. The juveniles learn what it means to be a victim and to appreciate what they have done to others. I have many positive responses from the juveniles who took the class as part of their probation. Jim is truly making a difference in the lives of the juveniles he teaches."

~ **Honorable Pat McArdle**
Gage County Judge

"Jim Jones is one of those rare people who get involved in crime, but are somehow able to make amends for the harm they have caused. More than anyone I know, who have harmed others, Jim clearly has given considerable thought to the consequences of his actions, and been able in a genuine way to acknowledge and address the harm he has caused to others."

~ **Gordon Bazemore, Ph.D.**
School of Criminology and Criminal Justice
Florida Atlantic University

GIVING BACK

The Community Justice Center Story

By James Jones with Jodi Fuson

Foreword by Anne Seymour

Giving Back

Notes of Gratitude

I would like to express my deepest and sincere appreciation to Jodi Fuson (co-author) for taking on this assignment and helping me capture the essence of my Restorative Justice journey. She made this long, detailed process enjoyable and was able to clearly share the spirit of my voice. I would like to acknowledge the financial support over the years from the Woods Charitable and Alice's Integrity Funds, and The Lincoln and Cooper Foundations. I would also like to give thanks to Linda Ulrich, Kent Krause, Tony Ojeda, John Krejci, Angela Mandl and Jill Shea for their editorial assistance.

I have to give special thanks to several Restorative Justice ground-breakers who have mentored me and who I've worked with over the past 25 years: Anne Seymour, Howard Zehr Ph.D., Gordon Bazemore Ph.D., Kay Pranis, and the late Dennis Maloney. They all welcomed me back into my community as a valuable stakeholder while encouraging me to develop the Community Justice Center's Offenders Motivational/Victims Impact Classes and the Victims First Team.

– Jim

I would like to thank my family for their support as I took on this book project, especially my husband, David. I would also like to thank my friend and fellow writer, Kent Krause, for agreeing to read the book and make suggestions for changes.

Finally, I would like to thank Jim for giving me this opportunity to help him put down his thoughts and share his passion for Restorative Justice. I was truly moved by his story, his transformation, and his passion for teaching his Offenders Motivational/Victims Impact classes. For additional background for the book I attended one of his eight-hour probation OMVI classes in Lincoln and was amazed at how effectively Jim related to the participants and how he was able to penetrate their defenses and get to the heart of their issues.

– Jodi

Dedication

This book is dedicated to all my direct and indirect victims whom I caused a great deal of harm, to include my wife Cindy, son Brandon, family members, friends, and my community.

I want to extend special appreciation to Cindy for the patience and understanding she has shown me for over 35 years of marriage.

Also, I am extremely grateful to a volunteer who I met in prison that gave me a priceless gift, a gift that I use and share daily. Finally, thanks to Gaylene and Jim Barstow, who inspired me to follow my dream.

Contents

FOREWORD

I am so honored to strongly support Jim Jones and the Community Justice Center's *Offenders Motivational/Victims Impact class*. This is a truly important program that helps offenders understand the impact of their actions on their victims, their own families, their community, and themselves.

The concept of victim awareness programming began over 35 years ago and has grown to become a basic and critical component of offender accountability programming. Far too often, crime victims and survivors report crimes and serve as witnesses in criminal and juvenile justice cases, yet feel that they are *still* not considered to be key stakeholders in our Nation's justice processes.

Jim, your Offenders Motivational/Victim Impact classes change this perception *and* reality. They bring to light the important fact that *crime hurts individual, real people*, and that victims' lives are forever changed by crime. They help emphasize the fact that our neighborhoods, schools, and communities are negatively affected by crime, and that in order to successfully reintegrate back into our communities, convicted and adjudicated offenders *must accept responsibility and accountability for their actions* and commit to improving their lives. Finally, they offer an important opportunity for offenders to examine themselves, the negative experiences in their lives that they can turn into positive actions, and how such positive actions can lead them down a path of responsibility, accountability, and good citizenship.

Jim, I salute you for your innovation and for this important program that unites crime victims and survivors, those who have hurt them, and our communities under one "umbrella" of justice for all.

ANNE SEYMOUR
National Crime Victim Advocate
Washington D.C.

Chapter 1

HARM

I failed again. *"F--- it!,"* I thought, as I headed for a local convenience store to rob it. I needed money for the crack dealer, and this was my only way to get it. Each time I ran out of money, I got back into my 1971 yellow Volkswagen Bug to rob another convenience store. I would hold my hand under my shirt and say I had a gun. Nothing mattered but getting that next hit.

I thought about how I had drained the checking account again buying crack and how I had been unable to kick my habit. You'd think after going through treatment after treatment program I would have figured it out. I knew I had let Cindy and Brandon down again. It was hopeless.

After my fifth robbery of the night, the police caught up with me as I headed west on O Street, back to the crack house near 27th and T streets. A female police officer pulled me over and I allowed her to search my car. She found the money I had hidden and immediately placed me in her cruiser. I knew it was over. I had to be stopped!

Riding downtown in the back of a police cruiser at 2:30 in the morning on October 3, 1989, I asked myself, *"How did I allow this to happen? How come I couldn't address my problems? What was wrong with me? I was supposed to make it."* My parents and step-parents did not raise a criminal; they taught me right from wrong. But now I was an incarceration statistic, whereby people of color (about 1 million) make up nearly 50 percent of the total number of people incarcerated in the country.

"How could I stoop so low to the point of committing robberies? When did I start thinking criminally? When did I say, 'It's okay to hurt people'? Who am I that I made this conscious decision? Was I a good person, and where did my values go? **Or did I have them in the first place?"**

The day before, I had gotten my grades from the Lincoln School of Commerce where I was taking business classes at the time. I was surprised to see my grades were better than expected, so I decided to celebrate with some cocaine. It was 1:00 P.M. I spent the rest of the day getting high, and by 2:30 A.M., I was in police custody.

My drug addiction began seven years before. I started out justifying my cocaine usage by only using at after-hours work events, but it quickly shifted to any event (negative or positive, perceived or real), sending me into drug binges. But this time was different. I remember saying that day, *"My life is over."*

In jail, my mind was racing over and over again thinking about all the damage and harm I caused the people who were working to take care of their families. *"How could I have caused so much*

**Jim's arrest photo
October 1989**

damage and hurt?" Then, my thoughts would shift to the other collateral damage I caused to my family, extended family and the 200,000-plus people of Lincoln. Now I had put the whole city of Lincoln in fear.

My wife, Cindy, and I had returned to her hometown of Lincoln, Nebraska, two years earlier with our son, Brandon. Brandon was just shy of nine at the time of my arrest, and Cindy and I had been married 10 years. I had promised my father-in-law before I married his youngest daughter that I was going to take care of her, and now I hadn't because of my cocaine addiction. Cindy's dad believed in me. He was a good man. I loved my in-laws, but I kept hurting them because of my inability to grow up. It felt like my whole world was coming down, but there was a sense of relief, too.

I didn't sleep at all that night in jail. A day or so passed before Cindy and Brandon came down to visit me. I'd never seen my wife so broken. As I looked at her and my son's eyes through the glass I said to myself, *"I'm repeating the cycle—now my son is going to follow me and the way I handle life. I have to break this cycle, but I became like my father, stepfather, and mother (alcoholics) but much worse — a crack addict and a felon."* I was directly and indirectly teaching my son the same self-destructive thinking and behaviors.

I can remember many events from my childhood. It was tough seeing the pain and hurt caused by the adults in my life who were abusing alcohol and drugs. I told myself that I was never going to cause this type of pain to anyone, EVER! As Brandon and Cindy left the jail, I thought to myself, *"No matter how much time I get in prison, I'm going to figure out what's wrong with me so my son will have a better chance of making it—IT STOPS NOW!"* In that moment, I started the habilitation process.

Restorative Justice concept starts to take hold

At the time of my arrest I was already beginning to get a sense of the concept of restorative justice—repairing HARM caused by crime. That's the guiding principle behind what I do at the Community Justice Center, a nonprofit public safety agency I founded in 2001 to address the needs of crime victims, offenders, and the community all at the same time.

Through my "Offenders Motivational/Victims Impact" class (OMVI), I teach offenders how they harmed their victims, families, and communities and help them see that they have an obligation to repair that harm. Seeing the true damage they've caused people and communities is a must. We go beyond that, though, and eliminate offenders' excuses and justifications for their behaviors and faulty decision-making processes. We start off with two basic questions—What harm was done? and What needs to be done to repair that harm?

**Cindy and Jim
Fort Riley, Kansas 1980**

That shameful night back in October of 1989 and my subsequent sentencing in January 1990 prompted a change in my life and my thinking. It started me on the road to growing up and owning up to events, emotions, and my actions. My inability to work through my emotions made it all too easy to blame others, make excuses, and justify my negative behaviors. I received a valuable gift in prison, a process for working through my feelings and picking positive ways to take care of problems. Now my passion is making my community safer by helping offenders discover the truth about what motivates them, how to process feelings, and how to understand the real impact they have on others (victims, families, and communities).

In the next chapter, I tell about my childhood and the years leading up to my arrest at the age of 29. I offer this as insight to how I developed my thinking patterns and began avoiding my feelings and making excuses to justify my behaviors. I know this is a common denominator among all addicts/alcoholics and offenders, both young and old. These attitudes and behaviors are directly tied to emotions. I want to help others who have similar backgrounds and inspire them to look at and work through their emotions so they, too, can reach their dreams and give back to their community, instead of taking away from it.

Chapter 2

LIFE'S NOT FAIR.
GET OVER IT!

After my arrest at age 29, I really started looking at who I was. The second oldest of four boys, I had been raised in an alcoholic family environment in the Washington, D.C. metro area. At age 25 my brother and I were shot during a drug deal gone bad. I hadn't been able to cope with my father's death at the age of 45, five years before, let alone financial problems, medical issues dealing with my back, finding work, or kicking my crack cocaine addiction.

My first memorable lesson in how to deal with emotions was around age 7 or 8 when my Uncle Eli yelled across his backyard for the neighborhood boys to come over because my older brother, Derrick, and I were going to beat them up. Uncle Eli didn't like them for some reason and forced us to fight them. We won, but I was hurting. My father said, "Don't cry — You can't let them see you are hurt." That's the first time I remember covering up my emotions. I also recall noticing guns behind Uncle Eli's apartment door and finding out he sold drugs.

My parents separated and divorced in 1963, when I was 5 years old, and my mom married Morgan, my stepfather. My biological father, JJ, wouldn't really be a part of our lives again until my last year of middle school. My mom's second marriage started out okay, but over the years she and my stepfather drank heavily. On Friday nights it seemed as if there was always a fight between them or whoever they had over. I told myself I was never going to end up in a relationship like that. I never wanted to be around people who screamed, yelled, or shouted. I can remember trying to cover my ears and praying no one was going to get hurt that night.

I have blank spots in my memory growing up, which I attribute to some of the violence and drinking going on around me. Life was unsure, and I was scared a lot. I believe that this is when I started avoiding my feelings.

I remember moving around a lot. We would sometimes stay at grandma's house when mom would leave Morgan. When we did move, my mother always moved into the same neighborhood or apartment complex as her older sister, Aunt Theresa, and my cousins Raynald, Shannon, and Gregory. We kids considered ourselves as one growing up. Raynald was the same age as me, and we all hung out together. My aunt was tough. Nobody messed with her. She was active in local government and the Black Power movement in the '60s and early '70s.

One of many frightening events occurred when we were staying with my grandmother. I watched my Mom get dragged for a block as she hung onto the car door while my stepfather, Morgan, tried to drive away with my youngest brother, Morgan Jr. After that, we moved to Palmer Park, Maryland, into our first house. I remember seeing Sugar Ray Leonard running in the neighborhood. I was still in elementary school and taking special reading classes. I felt isolated, and my brothers and I were teased because we didn't have nice clothes or basic things other kids had.

We were in the house for about a year before we ended up back in an apartment in Landover, Maryland. Most of the time mom was at home, but she worked from time to time for a linen cleaning service. I remember fights over money, and, of course, alcohol was involved. I went through my high school years in a two-bedroom apartment, with us four boys crammed into one bedroom.

Toward the end of middle school my biological father reappeared in our lives. He had remarried a wonderful lady from North Carolina named Helen. My father would pick us boys up for the weekends and take us to his home in Oxon Hill, Maryland. During this time, he would hang out with his friends, often drinking in liquor store parking lots. At times I felt he was educating us about the streets.

My dad was known as one person you didn't want to fight, and when he got intoxicated, confrontations always erupted. I often witnessed those fights, and I never saw my father lose. He was known for his hands and his power. The pain he inflicted was out of this world.

I started spending weekends at my dad's house with my step-brothers Larry, Victor, and Kevin and my half-sister Monique. Staying there was a lot better than Landover. There was some type of normalcy, even though alcohol was still an active part of day-to-day activities. I loved my mother and stepfather, but it was hard living in Landover. I learned later that my father's drinking was tearing his new family apart, too.

Back at the apartment, it seemed like the police would show up often because of the fighting or noise. A couple times a month there were knock-down, drag-out fights, primarily between my mom and stepdad. My stepfather's drinking partners would often stay overnight on the couch, and I'd sleep in the living room on the floor or on a second couch. It was hard to sleep with the stench of alcohol breath in the room. My last year of high school, I stayed away from home as much as possible.

At school I felt like I didn't really fit in or belong. I did okay — even if I didn't read well. I was a C student. One day, a guy in my apartment complex started talking to me about the military. I decided it was a way to get out and away from the drinking and violence. My junior year I attended classes at Fairmont Heights High School during the day and caught a bus to Bladensburg High School for a night class so I could graduate early. Often I went from night school right to work at a Roy Rogers Restaurant until 11 P.M. or 12 A.M. After my shift, I'd head home and take a bird bath in the sink and wash out my clothes for the next day. My brother, Derrick, and I would trade clothes because we were about the same size.

Before I graduated, I started talking to a recruiter and got my mom to sign papers so I could go into the military at age 18. In 1977 Derrick and I joined the U.S. Army. My cousin Raynald joined a year later. I was assigned to Fort Knox, Kentucky, for basic training and then went on to Fort Benjamin Harris, Indiana, for administrative training to become a company clerk. From there I was assigned to Fort Riley, Kansas, where I met my wife, Cindy.

Cindy, a fellow enlistee in the military, and I married in 1979, and Brandon was born in 1980. I was doing well, I thought. My military job was going well. I was awarded the Army Commendation Medal as well as named Soldier of the Quarter of the 541st Maintenance Battalion with the 1st Infantry Division, The Big Red One. Yet, I was always worried about my mother and younger brothers back home in D.C. Both Derrick and I would send money home monthly to help the family.

As a teenager entering into adulthood, I thought I was ready to take on the world. I could handle anything. Boy was I wrong. I was not prepared for what life was about to throw my way (back surgery, financial hardships, and my father's passing). I was not equipped emotionally to deal with life on life's terms. I clearly see now that learning to correctly deal with my feelings would have given me a better chance in the long run.

I planned on retiring from the military when I first enlisted, but a fall during a field exercise took me down a different path. I found out during my second year in that I had a lower back disc problem. It was very painful, but it wasn't bad enough for me to be medically discharged. I started taking pain killers. I completed my three-year tour and was honorably discharged from the military in 1980. After I got out, I worked as a loan officer for a nationally-known company doing skip tracing (finding people who moved and hadn't paid back their loans).

After Cindy was discharged in 1981, we decided to move back to her hometown of Lincoln, Nebraska. We had visited Lincoln several times, and I couldn't believe how clean and nice it was compared to D.C. My brother in-law, Rene, got me a job selling insurance. It took me three times to pass the state exam to get my license. It wasn't for me. I lasted about a year before moving on. I then became a security guard at the University of Nebraska–Lincoln, where I issued tickets and towed cars.

At 23, I thought the world was against me. I was fighting the Veterans Administration regarding my back, and I upped my intake of pain killers. My negative attitude made me start to dislike Lincoln. I tried to find better jobs but then started thinking that I would have a much better chance back in D.C. Another factor that made me decide to move back to D.C. was that my mother and biological father, JJ, weren't doing well health-wise. My father had split up with Helen, and alcohol was taking him.

I also missed being around people of color. I had lived most of my life in the D.C./Maryland area, surrounded by a large black population. Cindy was white, and so was Lincoln. I took it personally when people would call me the "N" word as I walked downtown. So, I convinced Cindy to move back to my hometown.

We both joined the D.C. National Guard. Cindy was hired as an administrative assistant to general staff, and I was assigned to one of the line units. Marion Barry was the mayor at the time, and the city was rampant with cocaine. Rayful Edmond, a notorious drug kingpin, flooded D.C. with massive amounts of cocaine. I believe it was known as the murder capital of the nation that year.

Soon after Cindy and I started working for the Guard we were invited to several events where high-ranking co-workers indulged in powder cocaine. I believed that cocaine was just a harmless social drug. That was Mental Error No. 1.

Once we were settled in, we got the news that my mother's and stepfather's lives had taken a turn for the worse. My mother had a blockage in her liver. I made Mental Error No. 2 after a long day of dealing with my back, trying to take care of my immediate family, as well as my mother, father, and brothers. I saw the cocaine all around me. It didn't seem to have any adverse effects on people's lives, I thought. *"These people aren't being hurt by this. They have nice houses, careers, and are making nice incomes. It's okay."*

In 1982, I started snorting cocaine and combining it with alcohol and pain killers the doctors had me on for my back. That deadly combination made trying to cope with day-to-day activities impossible. I was gone.

My drug usage hit a new level after I had back fusion surgery in 1984. Surgery made me unfit for retention in the Guard, so my full-time National Guard job went right out the window. I was still recovering from surgery, and financially things were a mess. Both parents were not doing well. I was lower than ever before.

When the doctors told me I needed to come off of the pain killers I'd been on since before my surgery, I upped my intake of cocaine. It became my substitute. I was anesthetizing myself to all physical and emotional pain. I was good at masking my feelings as a child, but now with crack cocaine, I was able to do it even better, so I thought.

About that same time period, my younger brother, Ernie, was a street runner, selling crack cocaine for Edmond's operation. One day Ernie was smoking crack instead of snorting powder cocaine, and he suggested I try it – Mental Error No. 3! I thought it was just a different way of using the cocaine. I didn't realize that it would have a more intense effect if smoked.

In the summer of 1984, I received a call from one of my father's cousins, whom my father lived with off of Florida Avenue in D.C. He said my father was taken to the hospital and that I should get there as soon as I could. Upon my arrival, I was told that he had passed. He was 45. We were friends as well as father and son. Earlier in the day, I had taken him to a doctor's appointment, and he had said he never felt better. My father had a bad heart. His funeral was the first I had ever attended.

The combination of trying to deal with all of life's ups and downs (zingers I call them) as well as his death was too much to handle. What hurt the most was that I don't ever remember telling my dad, "I love you." My cocaine usage increased 1,000 percent following his death.

In February 1987, I was a full-blown crack head. I went with my brother, Ernie, to an apartment off of Capitol Hill Extended (a neighborhood near RFK stadium that was an open air drug market and rampant with crack cocaine). He was going to get a package. My brother was also using heavily and messing up the dope man's money.

While I stood on the corner waiting for him to come out of the apartment, I watched guys shooting dice. Suddenly, I heard Ernie yell, "I got what you got" and look in my direction. Then the guy next to me pulled a gun out of his jacket and fired two shots at my brother, hitting him in his upper abdomen. I grabbed the shooter's arm and pulled it down to his side. It went off again, and a bullet entered my left hip and travelled the whole length of my mid-section, lodging in my right side. Everyone scrambled. I was able to get to the car and drive Ernie and myself to D.C. General Hospital a few blocks away, where we both underwent surgery.

I asked my cousin Raynald to get in touch with Cindy and tell her what had happened. She was so upset that she told him I could lie there and die. That dug deep. He picked her up anyway and took her to the hospital.

Before surgery, the doctor told me that I would be wearing a colonoscopy bag because people who get shot in the abdomen typically have severe intestinal damage. The next morning I woke up and felt for the bag and noticed I didn't have one. During rounds, doctors stopped in my room and shared with me that they had never seen anyone shot in that manner have no internal injuries or damage. One of the doctors went on to say, NOTHING WAS HIT, NO ORGANS — NOTHING! He explained they had taken everything out and looked very carefully before putting it back. He also said that if the bullet would have hit my femoral artery, I would have bled out in minutes. I was only in the hospital a couple of days, and then I was hitting the pipe again. Ernie was hospitalized much longer; the bullet found his lung. He, too, went right back at it selling and getting high.

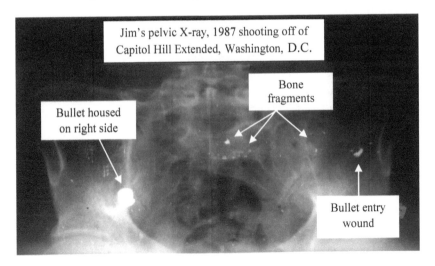

Jim's pelvic X-ray, 1987 shooting off of Capitol Hill Extended, Washington, D.C.

Bone fragments

Bullet housed on right side

Bullet entry wound

13

A couple of months after the shooting, Cindy decided she had had enough. We packed everything up and returned to Lincoln, thinking a new environment would help. A geographical move didn't fix anything. My problem moved with me.

We lived with Cindy's folks until we found work. I started going to Lincoln School of Commerce in downtown Lincoln. At the time, I thought that getting a degree would help. I even took a job at the city jail for a short period. Cindy called the jail and tried to tell them they had an addict working for them, but when they questioned me, I told them she was making it up and that we were having marital problems.

Cindy, my wife of 35 years, shares here how she was impacted by my poor decisions (harms) and my inability to process my emotions.

CINDY:

The day after Jim's arrest in 1989 I felt humiliation and shame. I went to work, and my coworkers were gossiping about the article they had seen in the paper about Jim's arrest.

Visiting Jim at the jail was a sad time for us. I remember looking through the glass at him and thinking, "How did this come to this point, because I knew this person I married was a good person and then this drug, cocaine, took control of him?" Then I started thinking about our son, who was not going to have a father because he was going to be incarcerated.

I didn't know the direction I was going to go. Do I continue with the relationship and bring Brandon down to the jail to see his father? Is that the environment you want your child to be in? I sought counseling for Brandon and me at the Child Guidance Center. My therapist helped me deal with the trauma of the situation.

I had so much belief in Jim. In D.C. cocaine had been a recreational drug. Jim was active with the Boy Scouts of America, the D.C. Youth Orchestra and the D.C. Youth Leaders Camps. "Was this drug addiction going to be what makes my marriage fall apart?" I asked myself. I knew Jim was a good person who started making bad choices.

When I was interviewed by investigators for the presentencing, I was able to tell them where all of the crack houses were because I used to go and get Jim. He was the only black man in Lincoln driving a yellow Volkswagen Bug, so he was easy to find.

At the time of Jim's sentencing in January 1990, I told my parents that I was going to stay with my husband. I remember sitting in the courtroom thinking, "If he gets more than 5 years, I will move on with my life. When Judge Blue said 3 to 5, I said, "I can manage that."

What I couldn't manage was living with an addict anymore. The only thing we argued about was Jim's drug habit. That, in turn, led to financial problems, the shame of filing for bankruptcy in 1986, and more arguing. There was no trust. If he said he was going out, my expectation was, "He's not coming back home". I couldn't trust him with money.

I started saving money for our first house while Jim was in prison. My first purchase was a VCR because Jim had sold ours to support his drug habit. While we were still living in D.C. Jim bought me a stereo system with top-of-the-line speakers that we couldn't afford. He was trying to make up for one of his binges. I told him to take them back because we had enough credit card debt. It didn't go back. It went to buy more drugs.

When Jim got out of prison, we went to counseling to make sure we knew what we wanted and what we should be doing. Shortly after his release, Jim ran into the brother of a drug dealer who offered to

> *sell him back our wedding rings. Jim had exchanged them for drugs on one of his binges. "We can get them back, buy them back," he said excitedly. I told him that the rings were dirty to me and threatened to call his parole officer. I made it very clear that I would not go down this path again."*

My unsuccessful attempts to kick my habit

From 1984-1989, I tried to stop using cocaine over and over again. I went through treatment several times at the local VA Hospital. They never really cared about me, and it was hard for me to understand "The Language." It was like trying to learn another language. I never was able to digest or apply what they were saying. Treatment is the most powerful thing that exists, but we need to figure out a better way of motivating addicts and alcoholics so they can truly understand and apply the tools necessary to succeed.

After 30 days of treatment I'd get out and say that I was perfectly fine — like most addicts. I'd go a few months without using, and then I'd have to crawl home and tell Cindy I spent all the money. Each time she'd say I needed to get help. I repeated this process of not dealing with my issues (emotions) and not dealing with life on life's terms right up to the robberies.

Then came that awful night of October 2, 1989, when I committed five robberies within about five hours. I had been clean for about a month or so when I ran across the coke man who had made a stop in Lincoln. I'd just gotten my grades after a hard semester at school, and I was surprised. I didn't feel I was going to get decent grades, but I did. They were great! It was time to celebrate! Like I mentioned earlier, any event (feelings, good or bad) would trigger my usage. All were dangerous to me.

I went to one of Lincoln's crack houses to buy some cocaine. I started getting high sometime that afternoon and didn't stop until my arrest at

2:30 A.M. the next morning. When I ran out of money, I told the dealer to wait and that I'd be right back with cash. That's when I entered the first convenience store and robbed it. I continued that pattern the next few hours each time I ran out of money. I was thinking, *"I've been through treatment over and over. My life is over — To hell with it."*

When the female officer pulled me over near 33rd and O streets, I didn't want to live anymore. I just didn't care. Nothing mattered. I was empty. Nothing was left of me, no consciousness — nothing!

I was doing what I've always done — avoiding my feelings just like I did as a kid. I stuffed them. I suppressed them, just like my alcoholic mother, father, and stepfather. As a child and in my youth I always thought I was going to make it out of what I called hell and beat the odds. Boy was I wrong!

In my opinion, one of the keys to reducing harm (crime) in our communities is to teach children early on how to work through their emotions so they can become emotionally proficient. This should be a required subject in schools, a critical competency taught early on. Helping young people in this way will do wonders in their homes and communities. This simple technique can help them get through life's ups and downs and avoid the excuses and justification games we play. This would greatly reduce a lot of self-destructive, self-defeating thinking and behaviors. Today, I can identify what's going on inside of me and process my feelings. That always benefits me, my family, and my community.

Following are reflections from some of the offenders who came to terms with their emotions and the harm they had caused after taking my OMVI class.

> **"It helped a lot on discovering the core and reasons of our decisions and actions, what we can do to help resolve the problems."**

"I now know how my victims were impacted and how to take full responsibility without pointing blame or making excuses."

"Made me understand how many people I've actually harmed, how I can do better and control/deal with emotions."

"It brought more insight into how the victims and community suffered from my actions more than I realized."

"It offered me new ways to look at my problems, starting with emotional issues (cause)."

I truly believe our communities would and can greatly benefit from teaching offenders, addicts, and alcoholics this method. We need to speed up the emotional growth process among these populations, but we have to speak a language they all can understand. I know we need punishment to a degree, but we also have to know when punishment is not working. What if we teach young people in grade school how to associate the six core feelings to events, basically showing them how to effectively process and express their emotions? It would benefit our communities 100 times over.

I learned how to become "EMOTIONALLY PROFICIENT" by way of a prison volunteer. She was doing prison ministry with a Christian organization and shared with me what I call The Million Dollar Check — "The Gift." She spoke a language I could easily understand, digest, and apply almost immediately. I still use this technique every day — 20-some years later. Some of us, like me, missed it growing up. Now I have a chance to share what that volunteer so kindly shared with me. I realize now that the source of my problems wasn't the pain killers or cocaine. IT WAS WITH ME and the emotional messes I hadn't cleaned up.

A lot of people have traumatic events happen to them in life, and they don't turn to drugs and/or alcohol to cope. Everyone on this planet will face difficult circumstances, such as a death in the family or medical and financial issues. Why couldn't I handle or deal with these issues like most people? Why did I choose a self-destructive path? It all came down to how I dealt with my emotions.

Chapter 3

CLEANING UP THE HOUSE — EMOTIONAL MESSES

Getting myself ready for sentencing was the most stressful time for me because of the unknown. I went up for sentencing right after the holidays — January 1990. I didn't want the state to waste any more time or money on me. I cost my victims and my community enough already. I wanted it over. *"Let me start my time. I was wrong!"* I thought.

One inmate told me to prepare for the worst, and others informed me that since I had a public defender for an attorney and because of the color of my skin, I would get at least five to 10 years in prison. Cindy and I talked it over. We decided that if I received a sentence longer than five years we would go our separate ways.

I appeared in District Court before the Honorable Judge William D. Blue and pled guilty to one count of robbery, reduced from five counts.

Judge Blue scolded me like a child and lectured me on how crack cocaine was destroying our communities. I was ready for him to lower the boom with a long sentence of up to 10 years. He looked at me and then looked down as if he had a second thought. When he looked up again, he said, "Three to five years prison." I could have gone up and kissed him square on the lips. He gave me back my life.

After Judge Blue sentenced me, I was immediately transferred to Nebraska Department of Correctional Services - Diagnostic and Evaluation Center (DEC). I spent three months waiting to be transferred to the general population at one of Nebraska's nine prisons. Before I went to prison, I never really realized the number of poor, minorities, and mentally ill people locked up, most of them with drug and alcohol issues. I, too, was under the influence, but I knew what I was doing. Committing my crimes was a conscious decision. If anyone tells you differently, they are lying.

Eventually, I was moved to the Lincoln Correctional Center (LCC), where I resided for about a year or so. Each day of my 30 months in prison I would think about the pain and damage I'd caused. I was hungry for anything that would give me the best possible chance to succeed when I got out of prison. My end goal was to be a positive father, good husband, and contributing member of my community again.

One thing I learned in prison is that we spend a massive amount of money to ensure public safety, but prisons primarily warehouse people (criminals) and do little to habilitate (to make capable) them. We spend over $68 billion every year on prisons here in the United States, with most of that money going to bricks and mortar, staff, and inmate medical costs.

Putting money toward assisting the populations that really need it (the poor, children, and mentally ill) could prevent crime and cut prison costs. Study after study shows spending the money upfront is well worth the investment in reducing future crimes.

Our nation is feeling the effects of overcrowding in its prisons, and soon we will have to address this issue. Some options are building more prisons, sentencing fewer offenders to prison time, and putting more money into crime prevention. We need to reserve prisons for people we are truly afraid of and use alternative incarceration programs for the ones we are just mad at. Currently, judges are limited by legal constraints. We need prisons, but we need to continually examine the best ways to habilitate offenders so they can succeed in society.

Teaching offenders young and old how to become **emotionally proficient** is one of the sections of my OMVI classes. It's one way I help them reintegrate back into their communities. I realize there are offenders out there who have mental health issues or who are just mad at the world. These offenders refuse to look at or admit they have issues because life dealt them a bad hand. These are the ones that are less likely to respond to habilitation efforts.

Lessons learned behind bars

I call what I offer through my OMVI classes "habilitation." I am teaching offenders something they didn't have in the first place how to process their emotions in a way that benefits them. I share with them a technique I learned from a 40-something Christian volunteer I met in prison. The technique is more powerful than I could have ever imagined.

The volunteer broke down emotions in a way that I could understand and taught me how to eliminate all the excuses that I used in the past to justify my usage. She explained that I needed to learn to deal with my life on life's terms and work through issues on an emotional level. I could tell immediately that she cared, which made the difference for me. She spoke a language I could hear, understand, digest, and apply.

I was able to apply her gift to my daily life immediately. I still use this technique today, and now it's my mission to share it with others like myself who have used cocaine, pills, alcohol, or anything else to cope with life.

While I was incarcerated, I started addressing my issues and applying what that woman taught me. It made my prison time 100 times easier. I was able to handle all the situations at home and all the negative experiences in prison. I would always remind myself, "*If I can handle this stress and anxiety here in prison, I can handle any situation on the streets.*"

One awful event in prison that is burned into my memory is of a young man in for a DUI offense who was assaulted. Several of us inmates told guards that this young man needed medical help following the incident. They moved him into a one-man cell, but he hanged himself shortly after the first nightly count. Many of the inmates clapped as the guards hauled him out on a stretcher in a body bag. I wish the institution could have intervened sooner to help this young man. This incident demonstrated to me that we need to improve our prisons and how we punish offenders. This young man paid with his life.

Yes, holding offenders accountable is a criminal justice issue, but we must also address the individual's emotional and physical needs (health/wellness). I believe the reason for our high recidivism numbers is due to those health and wellness needs not being addressed. The numbers say it all. Seven out of 10 inmates will get rearrested within three years after they are released from prison, with 50 percent of those going back to prison for new offenses. Research also shows that, on average, they will commit two additional crimes before they go back. We have to ask ourselves, "Is this true PUBLIC SAFETY?" We need to stop fooling ourselves. How can we make this system better?

The focus of my OMVI classes is habilitating offenders via crime victim's education. Many (not all) can be habilitated once they figure out their true motivations and master their emotions. Offenders' issues can be directly traced back to a life event/emotional issues they chose not to address. If we can teach offenders how to eliminate all justification/excuses on an emotional level, then we can show them how to deal with life on life's terms. They will succeed, we will have less crime in our communities, and the revolving door of prison will slow down.

Offenders have a major role in restorative justice process

There are thousands and thousands of successful former incarcerated persons out in our communities who have addressed their issues and stopped committing harm (crimes). What's the common factor they all have? They all learned how to effectively work through their emotions — always selecting positive outcomes to help them deal with life on life's terms.

I wish more successful ex-offenders would commit to going back into the prisons to guide incarcerated persons through the process of owning up to their mistakes and the harm they have caused. These individuals will also help offenders prepare for life on the streets. I tell people who attend my classes, "*It's your job now to come back inside and help others when you get out. You have to give back.*"

I know I took a lot from my victims, my family, and the community when I committed my harms (crimes), but I am doing everything I can to promote healing through restorative justice. Restorative Justice (RJ) is a national victim-centered movement aimed at repairing harm and restoring individuals affected by crime, including victims, offenders, and the community. In my classes, I begin by explaining what restorative justice is and then ask offenders what harm they caused and what they're going to do to repair that harm. Before and after each session I use a questionnaire to assess their understanding of their obligation to their victim and community, financial cost to their victim and community, and emotional damage they have caused.

Restorative Justice

Before Crime	Crime Occurs	Current System Punishment-Based "RETRIBUTIVE"	Restorative Justice Repair-Based
The Community (whole)	Stakeholders (victim, offender and community) are harmed, and relationships are broken.	Injuries still remain, and relationships are still broken.	Victims, offenders, and the community all benefit from the process. Harm is repaired to the greatest degree possible.

I use a vase illustration in my class booklet to help show participants what crime does and how restorative justice works. Before a crime occurs, the community is whole, like an unbroken vase. After a crime occurs, the victim, offender, and community are harmed and relationships are broken. With our current retributive system, the injuries are still present and the relationships are still broken. The victims go their way and the offender, theirs — both still harmed and damaged. There is little chance for healing on either side. With restorative justice, victims, offenders, and the community all benefit from the process, and harm is repaired to the greatest degree possible.

Daniel Van Ness, Vice President of Programs and Strategic Issues at Prison Fellowship International states, *"Crime is more than law-breaking. People, relationships and communities are injured. Justice must include healing and be more than punishment. Justice must include repairing the harm done to people, relationships and communities — they must be restored."*

During those 30 months I spent in prison, I tried to repair some of the harm I caused by staying involved in Brandon and Cindy's lives and focusing on my issues. They visited me weekly when I was in Lincoln and monthly when I was moved to the Omaha Correctional Center. I remember helping Brandon practice his math times tables through the mail and then working with him when he came to visit. The disconnect was really tough, though. At age 11, Brandon let me have it with both barrels when he told me that I wasn't his father because I wasn't there for him. IT KILLED ME INSIDE!

Near the end of my sentence, Cindy's dad was dying of cancer. One of his last outings was to come up to Omaha and see me. It meant a lot to me that he worked up all that energy to make the trip. I had a picture of him on my cell wall, and it fell one day. Little did I know it was a sign. I talked to Cindy later by phone and asked her if everything was okay. She told me that her father had passed that morning. I wanted to be with Cindy to console her, but I couldn't.

When a person does time, the family does time with them. Each time Cindy and Brandon came to visit, they were pat searched. Brandon was exposed to all kinds of scenes in the family waiting and visiting rooms. During my imprisonment, he struggled with his emotions and the baggage my addictions and conviction had left behind.

The clerks and businesses I robbed were not my only victims. That's why victim impact awareness is at the core of my classes. I want to help offenders identify everyone who has been affected by their crime (harm). Following is Brandon's recollection of how my actions affected him.

Brandon

I remember my mom telling me my dad was in trouble as she drove me to my cousin's house so we could walk to elementary school together. I went to school with that in the back of my mind. Eventually Mom told me he was in jail. We visited him a few days later and I remember seeing him through the glass and feeling angry and worried. I saw this guy broken and caged in a box.

I felt like I lost my dad. I kind of figured "Now is divorce time." Most of my friends' parents were divorced or in the process at the time.

Within the next few months I felt an "I don't care attitude" click on. If my dad could be bad and do whatever he felt like doing, why shouldn't I? I started rebelling. My mom was pretty good at keeping me in check, though.

Before my dad's arrest I knew he was doing drugs. I'd been on rides to Omaha with him where he'd sold stuff of ours (like our VCR) to get drugs. There were fights between him and Mom. She would hide money, and he would find it.

His arrest was a shocking awakening, a realization of how bad it really was. I felt ashamed. I didn't know how to tell my friends that my dad was looking at prison time. Around my mom's side of the family I wondered how they perceived me and my dad.

It was weird at first, watching him come to grips with being in prison. Then you saw his demeanor change. He came to terms with it and started this process of trying to better himself.

Shortly after dad was sentenced, we moved to an apartment. I had to get rid of my favorite dog, Shane. During the summer, I would spend a lot of time at my cousins because my mom worked full time. I remember getting birthday cards and Christmas cards from my dad that he drew. He'd use toothpaste to stick things on the card.

When dad was released, we started butting heads. I wasn't meeting his expectations, and I wasn't used to having him around. Listening to him giving orders at first wasn't easy. I felt like, "Dude, you caused a lot of problems. And who's to say you're not going to do it again?"

It took me about a year to appreciate him coming back. We just had to get to know each other again on a father-son level. I think the long-term impact of my dad's crimes is not having full trust in someone. I feel like anyone could lie to your face if they have a reason. At the same time, seeing my dad conquer his demons first-hand has helped me in my life tremendously.

Chapter 4

REENTRY — GIVING BACK

When I got out of prison in 1992, I had to slowly reintegrate myself back into the role of father and husband. I suggested to Cindy that we talk to an outside therapist when I was out on short furloughs to help with the transition. I found out that things would never be the same, but that if I dealt with my emotions effectively, I could now handle life on life's terms. It wasn't easy, but Cindy and I have now been married for 35 years.

My first job out of prison was washing dishes at Bonanza. I grappled with the fact that I had to earn my way back and that things weren't going to be the way they were before. Back at the Lincoln Correctional Center, that volunteer gave me another great piece of advice regarding employment. She told me to look for work that I liked when I got out. After some soul searching, I thought, "I like people", so I entered Southeast Community College's Human Services program to work with kids in the drug and alcohol field. For two years I held a full-time, third-shift job as a drug/alcohol technician at Center Pointe, a treatment center. During the day I took Brandon to and from school and attended classes.

In 1994, I received an associate's degree in drug and alcohol counseling with youth specialization. I quickly became disillusioned with the revolving door of the treatment process. Treatment is very important, don't get me wrong, but it didn't motivate me. It was very disheartening to see people dying and relapsing all the time and not succeeding in treatment. Based on what I saw, I started working with kids on a prevention and intervention basis at Lincoln Action Program (LAP), now known as Community Action. The nonprofit agency supports low-income families in becoming self-sufficient. I was hired through AmeriCorps, a national service program that allows individuals to serve in their communities and earn monies for school or pay back student loans.

I didn't think LAP would hire me because of my record. Who's going to hire a person to work with youth who was convicted of robbery, served prison time, and was a crack head to boot? But Gaylene Barstow and executive director Beatty Brasch saw my passion to help young people not end up in prison. I told them I didn't want kids to go through what I went through. Even to this day, Gaylene continues to champion my efforts at the Community Justice Center (CJC) by assisting with financial support and non-profit governance.

At LAP, I was assigned to the "Tutoring Program." Some of the kids were on probation, while others were at-risk youth. After about six months, I approached Beatty and Gaylene and asked if I could create a program that would help our kids learn about how crime hurts people and communities but at the same time assist crime victims. *"Why can't we take these kids and expose them directly to recent crime victims?"* I asked. *"Let's show them firsthand the harm crime causes people and communities and let's offer victims immediate help."* LAP secured grants from the Woods Charitable Fund (Pam Baker and Tom Woods) to support the "Victims First Team" that I coordinated for seven years.

Through this firsthand experiential learning program, I wanted to influence at-risk youth and youthful offender populations on a deep emotional level. I wanted to help youth who felt detached from their community to understand that they have value, that they belong and have something to give others. When they get that, they are much less likely to destroy their community.

Giving back leads to repairing harm

The Victims First Team was the birth of me giving back. Through the team, I practiced and perfected what I had learned in prison about processing my feelings.

Through their exposure to surrogate victims (not theirs), these teens learned how people and communities are harmed by crime as well as how to process their emotions. I started by getting names of victims from the newspaper and referrals from victim's organizations. Then I, or another staff member, would visit the victim, tell them about our program, and ask if there was any way we could help. If they said yes, (98 percent did), we took a team out the next day to complete what we called "The Victims Service Call." We would rekey houses, fix broken windows, help domestic abuse victims move, paint over graffiti, clean up trash, and mow yards — anything the victims wanted us to do within an hour or two (free of charge). I was fortunate to be able to bring Brandon and a couple of his friends on board as team members.

The Victims First Team had several goals, but the overriding two were helping victims (repair damaged property) and giving them a voice. A lot of times when crimes occur, victims are victimized twice, once by the offender and a second time by the system when the case is pled down. We wanted victims to feel their needs were No.1 and that we were there to listen and help them in their healing process on their terms.

Before I took the youth out, I explained to them what crime (harm) had occurred and what the victim's needs were. I especially made sure that they paid attention to the victim's feelings. In 1996, U.S. Senator

31

Bob Kerrey met with the Victims First Team to find out what the kids were learning from the program. He went to bat for us and secured a $550,000 earmark to expand the Victims First program, which allowed us to go out several times a week to help more victims. It was a busy three years and brought with it service on several committees and boards in the Lincoln area, including the Youth Detention Center Advisory Committee, Lincoln Lancaster Drug Project Board, and Nebraska Juvenile Justice Task Force.

The Victims First Team gave me the opportunity to flood the youth with a powerful experiential learning experience. I wanted them to feel they were just as important as the mayor, police, and fire department. We even had bright yellow T-shirts that served as our uniforms (later we changed to red).

Each time we went out, I instructed team members to document mentally what emotional, financial, and long-term damage the victims had experienced and would experience. After the team completed the work, the victims would share how they felt when they arrived home and found their homes broken into and property stolen and destroyed. I had the youth sit down and process our experience, explaining how the victim was harmed directly and indirectly and how the community was harmed. Afterward we would go to McDonald's and then do something fun, like play basketball.

I've incorporated a similar "processing" component in my Offender Motivational/Victims Impact class, requiring participants to read 10 victim's impact statements from the CJC website or newspaper articles over 10 days and record how victims and communities were harmed. These homework assignments reinforce what participants learned in class and how real people and communities are harmed by crime.

Four years into the Victims First Team program, I attended a Restorative Justice (RJ) conference put on by the United States Justice Department. An organizer told me, *"Jim, you're doing restorative justice work. You are addressing the needs of victims, offenders, and the community all at the same time and doing it in a unique manner that hasn't been done before.*" He went on to share with me that most jurisdictions around the country do RJ one way, which is known as Victims/Offender Dialogue (V/OD).

That was the first time I had heard the concept of RJ. I didn't know that what I was doing had a name and a history. At that conference I was also challenged to go back and compare the numbers to see if the kids I was working with were getting in trouble with the law more or less. The answer was much LESS! That RJ conference organizer had also asked me what my victim's satisfaction ratings were. I said 98 percent. He said, "*I know Jim, all RJ programs have high victim satisfaction ratings.*"

There are two experiences I had with the Victims First Team that stand out in my mind, still to this day. First, we were able to show emotional support to McDonald's employees by cleaning up trash shortly after a young man was fatally shot in the parking lot over marijuana. Another experience that had a deep impact on the team was when a burglary victim shared two photo albums of her little white dog with us. It was shot in the head during the burglary, and the owner was deeply traumatized. The dog was her baby, a family member. There wasn't a dry eye in the room when she finished. The kids were touched. I realized then that teaching kids how to process their emotions is just as important as teaching reading, writing, and arithmetic.

During this time period, U.S. Justice Department head Janet Reno was educating communities around the country about RJ and "Victim/Offender Dialogue" (V/OD) programs. The Justice Department held five regional RJ symposiums, touting its benefits and promoting its effectiveness. It was at one of these regional RJ symposiums that I met National Crime Victim Advocate Anne Seymour, who welcomed me, an offender, back into my community.

At a symposium in Portland, Oregon, I met several of the organizers, who recruited me as a presenter for the rest of the symposiums. Their reactions to my program were remarkable. They thought what I was doing was a powerful example of RJ in action, applied in a simple and unique manner. *"Jim, you are using surrogate victims and offenders to address the needs of both, as well as the community (increasing public safety),"* they told me. This was a big step, a phenomenal opportunity. It opened the door for me to attend the U.S. Justice Department National Institute of Corrections to become a Restorative Justice Trainer. Later I took additional courses — Advanced Restorative Justice Trainers and Restorative Justice Train-the-Trainer. Later that year I also attended the National Victim's Assistance Academy out of South Carolina, where I learned about victim resources and how to work with crime victims and survivors.

The Victims First Team helped hundreds during my stint as its coordinator from 1994 to 2001. They successfully gave victims a voice and a sense of control back. Many times we would hear, *"This is the first time anyone asked how I felt and what my needs were."*

We were on the right track, but there was more to be done. A meeting with one of my victims in 1999 would catapult me into taking the next step toward elevating victims' voices and promoting public safety.

**Brandon,
member of the Victims First Team
1995**

**Graffiti, Central Lincoln
1996**

**Asian Community Center vandalism,
27th Street, repainting basement
1998**

**Victims Service call following a robbery
at a convenience store, West "O" Street
1999**

The Victims First Team (Jim, back row, center)
receiving the Nebraska First Lady Award for
Community Service as a Group
1997

U.S. Senator Bob Kerrey
meeting with the Victims First Team
1996

Chapter 5

THE COMMUNITY JUSTICE CENTER

— THE DOOR

In 1999, while I was still at LAP, Mike D., the information technology specialist, had a conversation with the assistant in my office about me. He told her that seeing the name Jim Jones on my door bothered him a little. It prompted him to share details of the night he was robbed in October 1989. The assistant put two and two together and realized it matched my background.

The next day when Mike walked into my office, I thought he wanted to talk about a computer issue. Instead, he shared that he was struggling with what he had just found out about me. He started to tell me about the night a man named James Jones robbed the Texaco Station where he worked. Immediately I knew Mike was one of my victims.

We had worked at LAP together for two years before he mentioned any connection between me and that crack head who robbed him. To him we just had the same name. During our discussion, Mike shared the harm I had caused him and how simply seeing my name would bring back some of the memories of the night of the robbery.

During this informal Victim/Offender Dialogue (V/OD) meeting I was able to tell Mike how sorry I was for the harm I had caused him and his family when I robbed the Texaco station. I had wanted to apologize to my victims for years but knew I couldn't because if I approached any of them and they weren't ready, I could do more harm than good. Mike didn't even know that I had been released from prison.

I was able to put everything that I had been learning about RJ into that meeting with Mike. I answered some of his questions about that night and was finally able to come to the complete realization that I had hurt living, breathing people. All in all, it was healing for both of us.

What happened between Mike and me (V/OD) is recognized as the most effective RJ program in the U.S. A V/OD program is where a victim and the offender sit down and discuss the harm the offender has caused. The process is victim-centered and is done with a highly trained mediator as facilitator. Victims get answers and other information that may help them move forward on their road to recovery, and offenders get an opportunity to apologize, grow emotionally, and truly be held accountable to their victims for the harm they caused. Research shows that offenders who complete this type of RJ programming have fewer rearrests.

An obstacle to V/OD programs is that it can take months to set up the meetings, and many victims don't want to do a face-to-face meeting with their offenders. One of the biggest advantages the Victims First Team had was that we offered help the same week as the crime (harm) was committed. The victims we worked with wanted to share their feelings of anger, frustration, hurt, and pain. They didn't hesitate.

Victims have immediate needs, and all too often if the V/OD service is not offered soon after the crime (harm) is committed, most want to move on. The reason the Victims First Team efforts were such a successful restorative justice practice is we were able to address victim's needs immediately and be there to listen to them share their stories and feelings in a safe environment.

Replicating the door for victims to enter

That chance meeting with Mike D. was the catalyst for me to take the next step and found the Community Justice Center.

A couple of days after I spoke with Mike D., I began to think … *How can I replicate that "DOOR" with my name on it so my other victims can walk through it like Mike did? Why can't I create a "DOOR" where other offenders can put their names (after they have been through victims impact education), so their victims will know they are open to V/OD? Why can't I create a "DOOR" that allows victims quick access to victim's services information and a place to share their feelings anonymously with offenders? Why can't there be a "DOOR" where victims can find out if their offender has written an apology letter?*

After careful thought, I decided the Internet could provide all of those DOORs. The CJC website became a way to share information and resources safely.

From the research I had done and my work with the Victims First Team, I found that victims want to be validated, have their voices heard, and have access to resources. Through victim impact statements posted on the CJC Website, their voices are elevated, they gain a sense of control back, and healing can begin.

But I wanted to do more, so I took the basic concept of restorative justice that we used with The Victims First Team and the "The Gift" process I had learned from that prison volunteer and started developing a class for offenders that I call "Offenders Motivational/Victims Impact" (OMVI) class. It would help offenders come to terms with the harm they had caused, identify their value as a member of society, and show them the importance of cleaning up their emotional messes.

I wanted to impact offenders the way the Victims First Team members had been impacted during service calls. Instead of going to victim's homes and businesses, I had to go where most offenders are — in prison. I incorporated victim impact statements from the CJC website and newspaper articles to show them how crime really damages victims and communities.

Below are three Victims' Impact Statements from the CJC website that I have used in my OMVI classes as an exercise to allow offenders to practice identifying their direct and indirect victims and how they were **HARMED**:

> *"What was the crime? Her (my mother's) crime was "driving without a license", DUI, Drugs. How affected by the crime? The effects have increased over time. When I was little, she would leave me places and forget about me. When she was drinking or using, she never had time for me. When she would get caught by the cops, she would hide her drugs on me. She would forget to pick me up at school and she was physically and mentally abusive. She not only hurt me but, also hurt my brothers and sisters in this same way. I was their Mother when she was not around. They still count on me when they need something ... not her. I suffer because I don't have my best friend anymore ... my Mother. The one person I would try over and over to put all my trust into. There were good times when she was there and not using and she was a mother. I am so angry at her and hurt and ashamed. I still have not forgiven her and I'm finding it hard to."*

> *"I am a domestic violence victim (31-year old female). I was physically and emotionally abused. I suffered being grabbed, sat on, my son being called names and threatened. I was threatened in every way. I still have fear of the man who treated me like shit and I am angry at myself. I isolate myself from others and often I don't want to be around people and I always relive the events. I don't trust many people. I am trying to learn from this abusive experience. It took me away from my family and friends. To all women ... if you are in a relationship make sure you know your mate before you move in with him!"*

> *"I was raped over 20 years ago. I still cannot be alone after dark outside or at home without a gripping fear, especially when entering or exiting my car, or when stopped at a traffic light. Immediately after the incident, I felt that nothing was safe, nothing was normal or dependable. The police also made the situation worse. They interrogated me like I was a criminal. They didn't seem to want to believe me. I felt terribly let down by the people I was supposed to be able to trust. I lost a lot of my faith in law enforcement, too. But this was just another victimization which was caused by the original action of a rapist."*

The Community Justice Center is born

In 2001, I left LAP to start the Community Justice Center. A crack cocaine addict turned public safety advocate, I wasn't hesitant this time, as I was when I created the Victims First Team. *No one can tell me that I can't give back to my community, I thought. No one can tell me I don't belong. This is my community, and I can contribute to it. I caused a lot of pain and damage, and now it's my responsibility to repair that harm!* I have a saying I live by — "Have the courage to fail!" Living by this saying makes anything possible.

I'm often asked why I stopped doing my youth program. It's not that I've stopped; I've just expanded my work to reach many more victims and offenders, all while directly impacting public safety.

I started offering Offender Motivational Victims Impact classes (OMVI) within the Nebraska prison system as a pilot in 2001 with the permission of Harold Clarke, Nebraska's Director of Corrections at the time. *Would this work? Would this help incarcerated adults as it helped the youth I worked with?* I wondered.

The pilot program was well received at all three correctional facilities where I offered it: the Nebraska State Penitentiary in Lincoln, the Nebraska Correctional Youth Facility in Omaha, and the Nebraska Correctional Center for Women in York. It was later expanded to most of the prisons in Nebraska.

The key components of the OMVI class are:

1. Defining Restorative Justice

2. Defining Crime Victims

3. Offenders Self-Awareness — Becoming Emotionally Proficient, "The Gift"

4. The Cost of Crime to Communities

By 2006, a grant that funded the classes ran out, so I ended programming in Nebraska prisons for a time. That same year, I was approached by Nebraska Adult Probation. Adult Probation was starting up Reporting Centers (RC) to provide wrap-around services for high-risk offenders on probation. The CJC started contracting with the state to provide OMVI classes to adults and juveniles on probation in Lincoln, Bellevue, Omaha, Gering, Beatrice, Lexington, Hastings, Columbus, South Sioux City, and Norfolk, Nebraska.

Cindy Wohlers-Green, Reporting Center Coordinator, has seen the positive effects of the OMVI program on offenders on probation.

> *"The program motivates participants to ACTION and breaks down their denial systems. The class should be taken at the beginning of supervision. It opens their minds up to all Reporting Center programming and makes supervising them much easier."*

> **~ Cindy Wohlers-Green**
> **Lincoln Reporting Center Coordinator**

In 2012, we received additional funding to bring the OMVI classes back into prisons through a contract with Goodwill Industries and the Woods Charitable Fund. We now provide these powerful classes to all Reporting Centers and many probation districts across Nebraska on a "Fee-for-Services" basis.

I wanted to validate the effectiveness that I knew in my heart CJC OMVI classes were having on both inmates and individuals on probation. In 2012, The University of Nebraska – Lincoln, Department of Psychology conducted a Preliminary Program Evaluation of the effectiveness of the classes on adult probationary individuals. Dr. Dennis McChargue noted: *"The results were extraordinary. The outcome showed that OMVI class attendees were* ***two times*** *LESS likely to recidivate than those not attending the class."*

Among the OMVI class participants, over 60 percent showed some level of empathy and/or insight into the effect of their actions on the victim/community. *"These qualitative results are particularly interesting, given that the questions that prompted the responses were not designed to assess knowledge acquisition,"* McChargue wrote. CJC is now in discussion with the U.S. Department of Justice National

Institute of Corrections, which is looking at this data to see if it can be replicated at the national level.

When asked how the OMVI class was helpful, offenders in the York women's prison commented as follows:

"WOW, this was amazing. I needed to see the reality of how I have affected my victims and learn how to cope with problems."

"It made me realize how I hurt my victims and that it wasn't just one victim involved."

"(It helped me) to understand victims are important; it isn't all about me."

"I learned to use the process of identifying my issues, feelings and solutions to make better decisions."

Many people may not see how victims are still at the center of what I do every day considering that 70 percent of my time at the CJC is spent conducting OMVI classes. But through my classes, I'm giving victims a voice by using surrogate impact statements and holding offenders accountable for the harm they have caused. At the CJC we are addressing the needs of victims and offenders and restoring both to the community; and ultimately, we are increasing public safety, the overarching goal of the CJC.

I have been restored to my community beyond what I could have imagined. I currently work hand-in-hand with the Nebraska Correctional Institution I spent 30 months housed in. In 2009 I received the Sertoma Club's "National Service to Mankind Award" for my work assisting crime victims and offenders. At the awards ceremony I met the Honorable Pat McArdle, a judge from Beatrice, Nebraska, who was also honored with a national Sertoma Club award that year. He later approved the CJC to provide OMVI classes to youthful offenders from his district. Judge McArdle saw the value in what we were doing with our OMVI classes and sought to bring the program to his community. Now I want to help others bring it to theirs.

Chapter 6

Changing the Language

My way of giving back for the harm I've caused is helping others like me understand "The Language." When a person is arrested we ask ourselves, *"What law was broken?"* and *"How are we going to punish the person?"* RJ goes beyond that to asking, *"What harm was done?"* and *"What needs to be done to repair that harm?"* Changing the language this way will propel us much faster to reduce crime, promote safer communities, and save tax dollars.

During the first few hours of our OMVI class, we build trust and rapport as participants share their names, family information, and offense (harm). We address program goals, class objectives, and expectations, too. Once we establish those, we move on to defining restorative justice, using a language that they can understand, digest, and apply. That's why I believe we get such a good response compared to other traditional offender programming.

As I stated in the last chapter, helping participants understand the concept of RJ allows them to identify with their community. When they understand RJ, their guards come down, and they are ready to fully accept the harm they caused their direct and indirect victims and hear the victim's voices. This is where we communicate clearly the damage caused to their victims and help them take ownership of their "HARM." In an effort to get this key component out to more offenders, we are launching an online class in 2015 called Crime Victim Definition/Impact Class, whereby offenders across the nation can experience a segment of the OMVI class and gain an understanding of who their victims are and how they were hurt.

One unique thing about my classes is the peer-to-peer interaction between participants. Listening to others often helps them gain new perspectives about the harm their crime has caused. When a peer is holding someone in class accountable, they hear it 10 times faster. In one class a woman refused to take responsibility for the harm she caused, but her classmates wouldn't let her off the hook. I didn't have to say a word. The participants are quick to let a classmate know if he or she does not own up to his or her actions or if he or she is including something in his/her apology letter that might cause more harm to the victim.

In a recent class of 14, we had participants charged with driving while under the influence (4th offense), possession of a controlled substance, and assault and battery. They were the lucky ones who had avoided going to prison for their offenses and were on probation or enrolled in the Nebraska Specialized Substance Abuse Supervision (SSAS) unit. More than half of the group had kids, so I explained that their kids are seven times more likely to end up as they have or worse, in the penitentiary, because of the way they think. Many participants share that their kids are already in trouble of some kind, and many have had mothers or fathers who have been in prison or under some kind of community supervision.

After we share the victim's awareness piece and help participants see how they can take steps to correct the harm done, we move on to the "Offender Self-Awareness" section. We walk through what motivates them, how to deal with their emotions on life's terms, and how to understand their worth as a human being. We also share a foolproof, 100 percent guaranteed technique that will benefit them, if used correctly. I call it "The Gift." It's a three-step method we perfected to help offenders work through their emotions. There is nothing new in what I teach offenders in my classes. I just use a language they can understand.

Eliminating excuses and justifications, the first steps to dealing with emotions

Many criminals and addicts tend to act out of emotion, but they don't even know where those emotions are coming from. It is important to identify problems, events, or issues and work through the emotions associated with them. The goal is eliminating their excuses and justifications. When you take those off of the table, it changes their focus. Like a laser beam, it guides that person on their healing journey while helping them grow up. In turn, they can become a contributing member of society and stop causing harm.

More than 80 percent of all offenders report they were under the influence of drugs and/or alcohol when they were arrested, but the problem isn't with the drugs or alcohol. It is my belief that their problems begin with not learning how to effectively deal with their emotions, which translates to the choices they make. In class, we make a real emotional connection with attendees to accelerate their emotional competency development.

Offenders learn that they can actually deal with their emotions like most successful adults. I call it my pay day when I see a participant recognize the harm he or she has caused, grasp his or her value as a human being, and understand how he or she can deal with life's ups and downs, no matter what comes the participant's way. There's nothing like it.

For those who are ready to listen and able to digest what I have to share, I see a big change from the beginning of my eight-hour class to the end. Many walk in the door in the morning pissed off because they have to pay $125 and spend all day in class with me. At the end of class, many participants come up and thank me. They go home with a new realization of how they fit into society and the positive impact they can have in the future if they apply what they learned in my class.

Many parole/probation officers tell me that those who have attended an OMVI class through the CJC are more motivated, more willing to participate in other programming, more open to treatment, and easier to supervise. In turn, the likelihood of them returning to prison is reduced.

I truly believe that when you have that sense of belonging to a community you do not <u>destroy it.</u> Individuals can learn to take back ownership of the community even if the community doesn't accept them. I tell offenders who say, "I don't belong" or "I don't have anything to contribute" that they are full of it. I tell them they can make a positive impact; just start giving back. Start anywhere that would have you. Of course, society still has a right to verify their intentions, but they would want to do the same if the roles were reversed.

The common thread for the ones who don't reoffend is that they grow up on an emotional level and eliminate all excuses and justifications for their criminal behaviors. They learn to own their feelings and positively work through them (actions). Then they can be more successful putting things back into place, like working, going to school, and being responsible to their families and communities. "The Gift" teaches them to stay on top of their emotions and out of the "poor me" mode. For some, it's easier to go back to prison than to work through the emotions and clean up old problems. Prison is no big deal. It is the norm for a lot of offenders, not a deterrent.

The cost of sending people to prison is an extra burden on society, and one that continues to grow. On any given day, more than 5 million people are under community supervision in the United States and 2.1 million in prison.

According to a study published in 2012 by economist David A. Anderson of Centre College in Danville, Kentucky, the annual cost of crime in the United States for one year is now about $3.2 trillion dollars. The burden of crime exceeds the $2.7 trillion a year spent on healthcare by half a trillion dollars. "Quantifying these enormous costs," Anderson adds, "provides a strong rationale for prioritizing activities that deter criminal activity, including increasing the presence of law enforcement officers and improving education efforts and social programs."

The focus of CJC programming is to deter criminal activity (repeat offenses). These comments from OMVI class participants indicate the significant impact we are having.

> *"It taught me that I am somebody and can do good things with my life regardless of what I've done in my past."*
>
> *"It helped me to realize not only I was the one who was impacted but the victims were more impacted and violated!"*
>
> *"It made me realize how I affected my victims in the past and how we can restore the harm."*
>
> *"I was able to identify ways to deal with my anger and understand what impact I have on the community and the victims of my crime. Very upfront and constructive instruction was very beneficial to my learning style. THANK YOU SO MUCH!"*

With thousands of inmates being released from US prisons every year, our communities need to take steps to help them get reintroduced into society. As an agency, the CJC is helping reduce crime, increase public safety, and save tax dollars. We continue to reinforce the positive outcomes of our classes at national conferences, such as American Probation and Parole Association conferences.

Lincoln Day Reporting Center
Lincoln, NE
2010

Nebraska Correctional Center for Women
York, NE
2002

Jim assists a participant with his apology (HARM) letter

Jim tells participants how to clean up their emotional messes

Sharing the results from Dr. McChargue's evaluation of our OMVI class's impact on recidivism rates is one of the most rewarding and exciting experiences I've had. The results, which are being finalized and published, also show that the OMVI program has led to fewer staff/offender issues and safer institutions. The number of individuals we help stay out of prison more than pays for the cost of the CJC's programming. See recidivism statistics below.

Because of the success we have had statewide with our programming, we plan to expand it on a national basis. We have already been approved to do programming in California, Virginia, and Maryland when funding is secured. A list of our other products and services is listed at the end of this chapter.

Reducing Crime

Incarcerated Individuals – Recidivism Rates
Offenders Motivational/Victims
Impact (OMVI) Class Outcomes

A recidivism project conducted by the Community Justice Center with data from Nebraska Department of Correctional Services found that between 2001 and 2013, a total of **1,262** inmates participated in and completed the OMVI class. When they were released, within three years **10** percent* returned to prison for new crimes and **11** percent for rule (parole) violations for a total recidivism rate of **21** percent. The U.S. three-year recidivism rate is around **50** percent.

*Note: Our three year recidivism rate for new crimes does not include "A" sentencing offenders. These are individuals who are re-arrested for a new offense while on parole; their old and new sentences are combined. At the time of this project these numbers were not available.

Probation Individuals - Recidivism Rates
Offenders Motivational/Victims
Impact (OMVI) Class Outcomes

A 2012 University of Nebraska-Lincoln program evaluation of individuals under Nebraska Probation shows that **32.2** percent of those taking the Community Justice Center class recidivated (reoffended), while **68.5** percent of those in the control group recidivated.

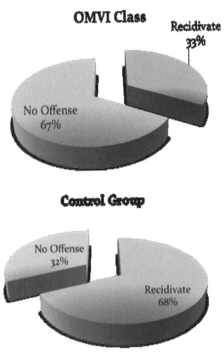

What we ultimately do at the Community Justice Center is help repair the damaged relationships caused by crime. When crime is committed, offenders sever the relationships between them and their victims and/or community first, and break the law second. I believe we need punishment and accountability. But what if our criminal justice system — from police officers all the way up to judges — changed the language a little? What if in addition to asking, *"What law was broken?"* and *"How should we punish the offender?"* they asked, *"What harm was done and what needs to be done to repair that harm?"* This paradigm shift would go a long way in addressing the real harm caused by crime. At the same time, it would elevate victims to their proper place within the justice process rather than being a secondary thought, and offenders would truly be held accountable while also having their needs addressed.

This change in language starts the process of restoring broken relationships between individuals and their communities. In the end, we must balance the needs of the criminal justice system, as well as the health and wellness needs of victims, offenders and the community, with the needs of the victims addressed first and foremost. This is the only way the core problem of crime is ultimately addressed. Habilitated individuals equal less crime and safer communities.

I've come to terms with the harm I caused my victims the night I committed my robberies in October 1989. I caused a lot of financial and emotional harm in their lives as well as in the lives of my wife, son, and the community of Lincoln.

By applying the concept of restorative justice and processing my feelings correctly, I've been given a valuable gift that has restored me to my family and community. If you're a person who caused harm, it's your obligation and responsibility to repair that harm — to the greatest degree possible. I hope sharing my restorative justice journey will inspire you to make a contribution to your community.

I also want to help other communities experience the same successes I have had at the Community Justice Center. Our products and services, including training on how to start a "Peer-to-Peer" Offenders Motivational/Victims Impact (OMVI) class (program) in your community, are listed on pages 60–63.

A friend sent me this quote by Hans Selye that I would like to close with:

"A long, healthy, and happy life is the result of making contributions, of having meaningful projects that are personally exciting and contribute to and bless the lives of others."

Promoting restorative justice through the CJC and teaching offenders how to deal with life on life's terms through my OMVI classes has been my way of blessing others and giving back.

**Cindy, Jim and Brandon,
Washington, D.C.
1983**

**Brandon, Cindy and Jim
Lincoln, NE
2014**

**Lincoln Police Chief Tom Casady receiving the
2010 CJC Public Safety Award**

Community Justice Center (CJC)

PRODUCTS AND SERVICES

Survivors/Victims of Crime Website Services

CJC creates a safe place for survivors/victims of crime and concerned citizens to anonymously share with offenders how they were harmed by crime. Over and over again we hear individuals affected by crime say, *"I DON'T HAVE A VOICE, MY VOICE WASN'T HEARD!"* CJC helps correct this problem through our website, which allows individuals to share their feelings and stories about how they were harmed by crime. We share these powerful stories during Offenders Motivational/Victims Impact classes. These stories have another important role because they are also read by other survivors/victims of crime, helping these individuals on their road to recovery. These voices are helping CJC hold offenders answerable for the harm they caused while helping other survivors/victims of crime know *"YOU ARE NOT ALONE!"*

If you would like to share your voice (A Victims Impact Statement) or need victims resources please visit our website at:

www.communityjusticecenter.org/crime-victim-resources/

CJC Presentations

Motivating Adult and Juvenile Offenders to Action Utilizing Surrogate Crime Victims: (90 minutes)

Attendees learn about the CJC's unique, non-traditional Restorative Justice (RJ) programming proven to motivate offenders to action. CJC utilizes surrogate crime victims to lower offender recidivism rates. This RJ approach is an important element in the habilitation process of offenders while increasing public safety! It concludes with data-driven research conducted by the University of Nebraska–Lincoln that illustrates how the CJC's approach is effective at improving institutional and community safety while lowering recidivism rates.

Audiences: Probation/Parole, Correctional and Civic Organizations

"Giving Back" Institutional Presentations (2 hours)

Jim gives a short but powerful presentation in which he shares his personal story with inmate populations in jails and prisons across the country, stimulating others like himself to really look at themselves and to see how imperative it is for them to **"Give Back."** This inspirational and thought-provoking presentation motivates individuals to change.

Audiences: Inmate populations - jails/prisons

Adult/Youthful Offenders Programming

Offenders Motivational/Victims Impact (OMVI) Class – Prison, Probation/Parole: (8 hours)

This Restorative Justice/Crime Victims Impact-based curriculum is for incarcerated persons and individuals on probation/parole. This class, which focuses on empathy for victims of crime, also provides offenders an effective tool to help them successfully transition back into their communities. The program reduces future crime while increasing public safety.

"The Vegas Technique" Offenders Employment Soft Skills Classes: (4 hours)

This half-day program provides individuals with criminal histories (misdemeanors and/or felonies) a step-by-step process to effectively secure employment in two weeks or less! The class covers data-driven/evidence-based job search methods and techniques, applications/resumes, and interview skills. These techniques can be applied to any barriers to employment.

Crime Victims Definition/Impact Class (CVDIC) – Online: (2 hours)

This powerful victim's definition/impact class is designed as a low-cost and easy access program for all offenders under community supervision. Those who complete this class will be able to identity their direct and indirect victims and the related damages the victims suffered because of their actions. This class is also used as a refresher course taken by individuals one year after completing the eight hour OMVI class, prolonging the effectiveness and working as a "booster shot."

Launching 2015

Youth Crime Prevention/Conflict Awareness Class

Youth Crime Prevention/Conflict Awareness Class:
(10 participants, 8 hours)

Jim provides a powerful Crime Prevention/Conflict Awareness program for youth 13 to 18 years old. It covers all aspects of how crime damages people and communities. The class also provides young people with valuable tools, such as how to become proficient in expressing emotions and understanding sources of conflicts.

Corporate Workshop Presentations

Reducing Workplace Conflicts – Understanding Sources of Anger: (2 hours)

This workshop provides staff with an effective tool that allows them to *instantly* identify a person's source of anger! Understanding the underlying source of conflicts is all too often overlooked when reconciling workplace hostilities. When the source of the dispute is validated and acknowledged, both parties can implement meaningful and positive corrective actions – resulting in fewer conflicts in the workplace. Jim provides staff with a clear step-by-step guide that helps employees develop awareness of and resolve conflict-associated emotions.

Contact Information

James Jones, Executive Director
The Community Justice Center
5625 "O" Street #114
Lincoln, NE   68510
(402) 429-1050
jjonesoasis-ne@neb.rr.com
www.communityjusticecenter.org

About the Authors

Presently, Jim serves as Executive Director of the Community Justice Center (CJC), a nonprofit, public safety organization he founded in 2001. The organization simultaneously addresses the needs of crime victims, offenders, and communities via its Web-Based Victims Services and Offenders Motivational/ Victims Impact classes. CJC elevates crime victims' voices within the criminal justice system (restoring control back) and assists victims  on their road to recovery. The CJC holds offenders accountable while building their competencies to reduce crime. Since 1994, Jim has been sharing "The Gift" with adult and juvenile offenders — teaching them how to become emotionally proficient and at the same time motivating them to change. He instills the God-given truths that each person is IMPORTANT, that each has VALUE, and that each BELONGS! God doesn't make any trash!

Jim began working at Lincoln Action Program through AmeriCorps in 1994. The Victims First Team that he created was recognized nationally as a model program that uniquely applies the principles and values of Restorative Justice in a meaningful and powerful way that truly increases public safety.

Jim's passion to give back to the community, while helping both survivors of crime and offenders, comes from his own experiences with crime. In 1999, Jim attended and received Victims Assistance Training at the University of South Carolina-Medical Center National Victim Assistance Academy.

Jim has served on numerous youth-focused and anti-gang advisory committees and boards in the Lincoln area. In 1998, then Governor Ben Nelson appointed Jim to Nebraska's Juvenile Justice Task Force.

Jim presents at Criminal Justice and various Restorative Justice Conferences around the country and has worked as a consultant for U.S. Justice Departments — National Institute of Justice (NIJ) and National Institute of Corrections (NIC). Jim received a full pardon for his crimes from the State of Nebraska in 2002.

Jodi Fuson is a freelance writer whose articles have appeared in *Women's Edition, L Magazine, Doane Magazine, Star City Sports,* and *Neighborhood Extra.* A former staff writer for the *Lincoln Journal Star,* Jodi and her husband David have resided in Nebraska for twenty years and have four children.

Jodi graduated from the University of Wisconsin-Eau Claire with a Bachelor of Arts degree in communications. This is her first book project.